THE ELLIPSE

THE ELLIPSE

BY MANNIS CHAROSH

ILLUSTRATED BY
LEONARD KESSLER

THOMAS Y. CROWELL COMPANY   NEW YORK

YOUNG MATH BOOKS

Edited by Dr. Max Beberman, Director of the
Committee on School Mathematics Projects,
University of Illinois

L.C. Card 73-132293
ISBN 0-690-25856-9
0-690-25857-7 (LB)
1   2   3   4   5   6   7   8   9   10

YOUNG MATH BOOKS

THE ELLIPSE

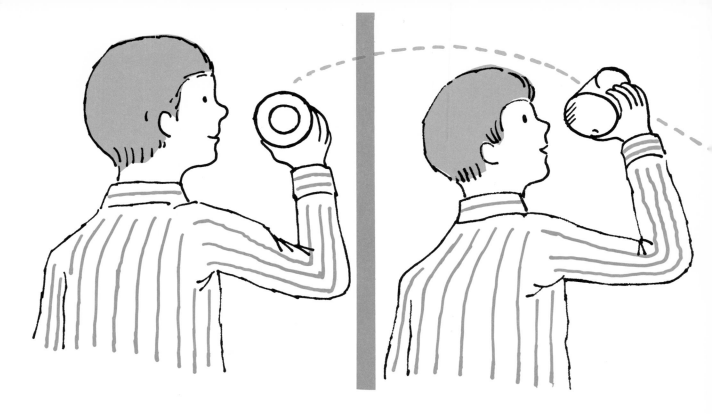

The rim of a drinking glass may seem to have many shapes. It depends upon how you look at it. If you hold the glass sideways and look directly into it, the rim looks like a circle. If you tilt the glass back slowly to its drinking position, the width of the circle —from left to right—remains the same; but the circle seems to flatten from top to bottom. This new shape is called an ELLIPSE.

As you tilt the glass more and more, the ellipse looks flatter and flatter. You can make the rim look like a straight line segment. Just keep tilting the glass until the top and bottom of the ellipse come together.

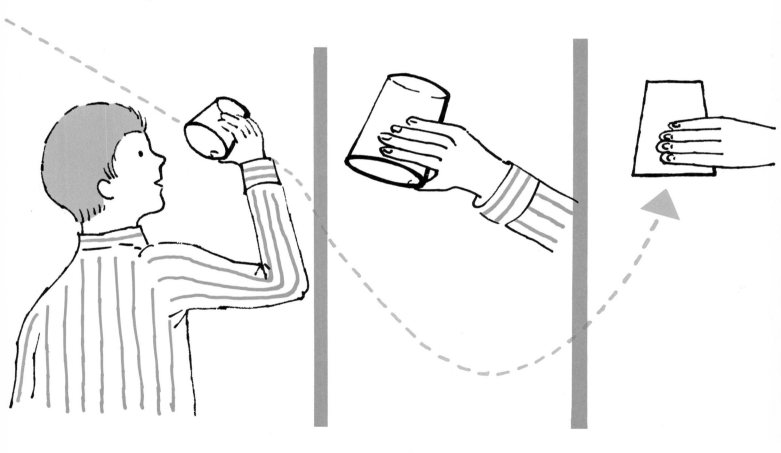

If you then keep on tilting the glass, the straight line will open up into a flat ellipse. Then it will open more and more from top to bottom. When the bottom of the glass faces you, look at the rim through it. The rim will again look like a circle.

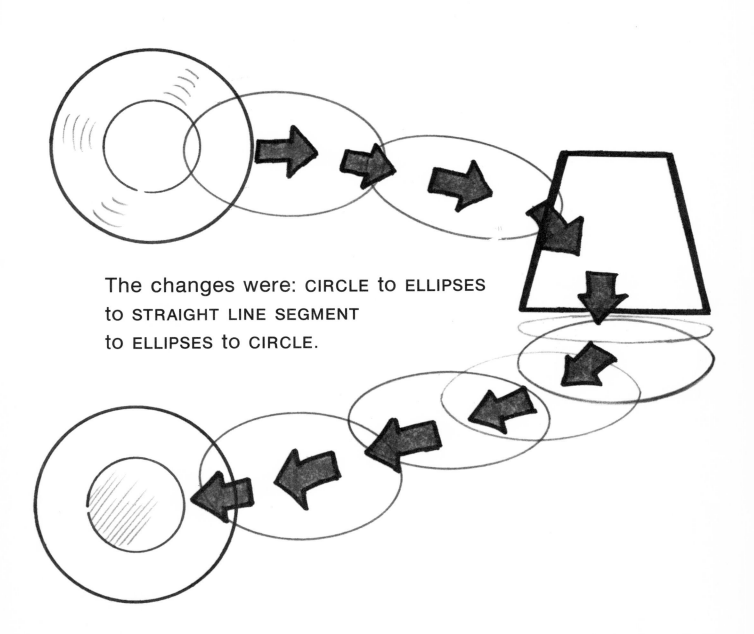

The changes were: CIRCLE to ELLIPSES
to STRAIGHT LINE SEGMENT
to ELLIPSES to CIRCLE.

3

Circular things often look like ellipses to us. This is because they are in a tipped position. The shape of a saucer is a circle. But if you place one on a table, walk away, and look back, it looks like an ellipse. As you walk closer to the saucer the ellipse will seem to open up more and more. When you reach the table and look straight down on the saucer, it will look like a circle.

Do you have a clock whose face is shaped like a circle? It may be on a shelf, or on a dresser, or hanging on a wall. If you face the clock from the front, it looks like a circle. But if you walk to one side of it, the circle seems to change to ellipses that get narrower and narrower.

Try to see the same changes in other objects
that are shaped like circles.
Here are some:

The dial on a telephone

A picture or mirror on a wall

The wheel of a car

A hula hoop

Some things are made in the shape of an ellipse.
If they are tilted, they can be made to look circular.

Some mirrors are shaped like ellipses.

So are some picture frames.

The knob on a classroom door may be shaped
like an ellipse.

The tops of some cans of fish are shaped like
ellipses.

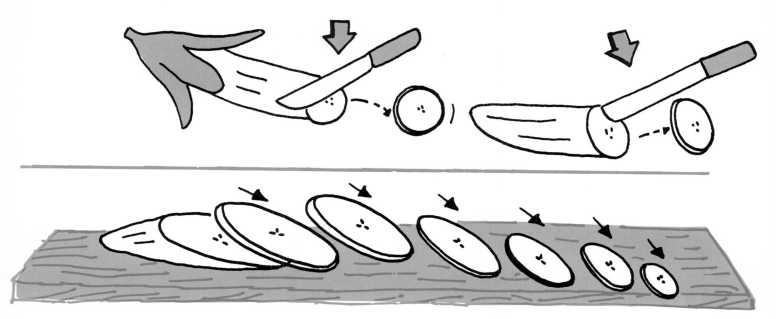

The shape of a slice of banana is sometimes an ellipse. If you cut a banana straight across you may find that the shape is a circle. But by cutting down on a slant you will get a slice shaped like an ellipse. If you keep cutting slices and turn the knife more and more, the ellipses will get longer and longer.

Let's draw an ellipse inside a rectangle.
First draw the rectangle carefully.
Then draw a line segment from the middle of
the upper edge to the middle of the lower edge.

Now draw a line segment from the middle of the left edge to the middle of the right edge.

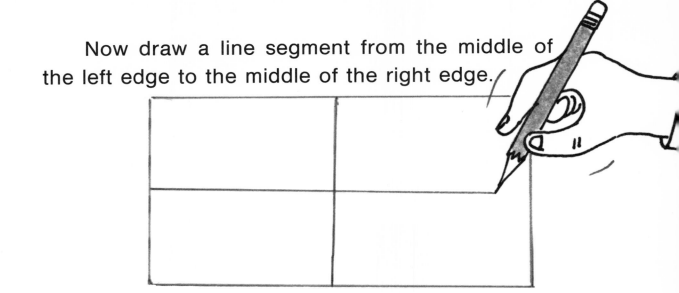

Draw small curves or arcs at the points where the dividing lines meet the edges. They will help you start the ellipse.

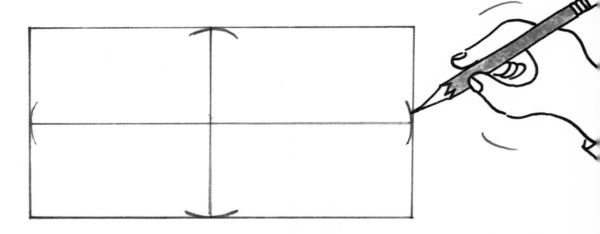

You can now finish the ellipse by connecting the arcs as smoothly as possible.

There should be no sharp corners in your ellipse.

If you want an ellipse that is longer up and down than right and left, start with a rectangle that is longer up and down than right and left. Go through the same steps as before. Or you can just turn the first ellipse on its side. Does the shape of this ellipse remind you of a face?

See whether you can put in eyes, a nose, a mouth, ears, and some hair. Of course no face is shaped exactly like an ellipse. But if you begin with an ellipse, it will help you draw a better face.

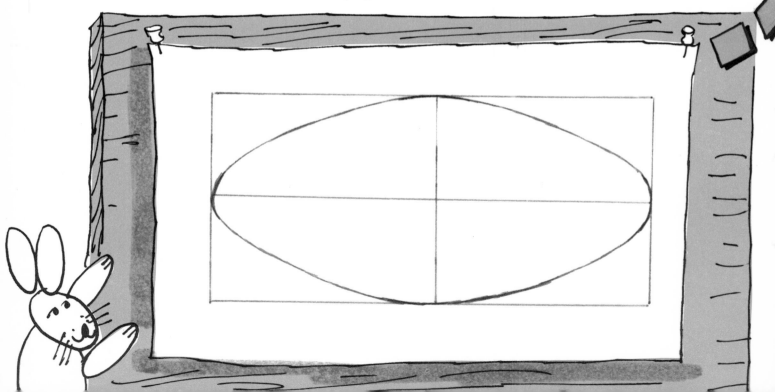

13

Try drawing ellipses in different rectangles: tall and thin, short and fat.

Your ellipses are probably not shaped exactly right.

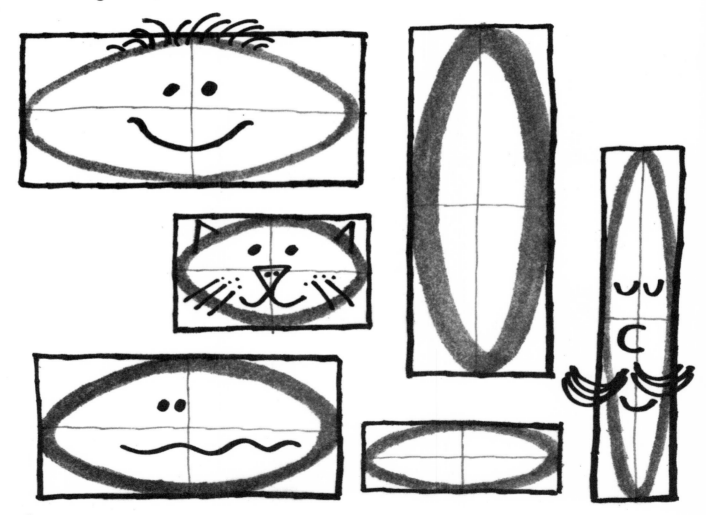

You can draw better ellipses with the help of a string, two thumbtacks, and a ruler.

We are going to draw a lot of ellipses on one page. First place a ruler in the middle of a large piece of paper. Hold the ruler so that it reads from left to right. With a pencil, mark dots on the paper near the marks for 1, 2, 3, and 4 inches on the ruler. Now mark a dot halfway between the first two dots.

Then mark another dot halfway between the second and third dots. And then mark another dot halfway between the last two dots.

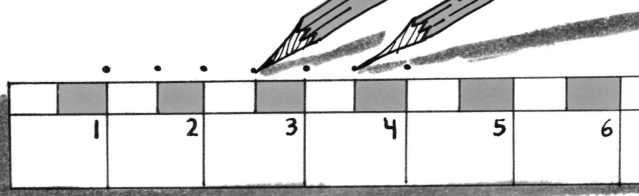

You now have seven dots. Remove the ruler. Then write 1, 2, 3, 4, 5, 6, 7 under these dots, beginning with the first one at the left.

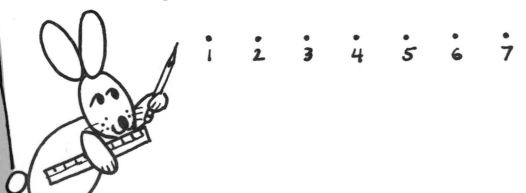

Place the piece of paper on top of a thick news-paper. Then push thumbtacks into the dots marked 1 and 7. With a string, tie a loop around the two thumbtacks. The loop should be a little loose. Now pull the loop tight with a pencil held inside the loop. Move the pencil around the tacks, keeping the loop tight.

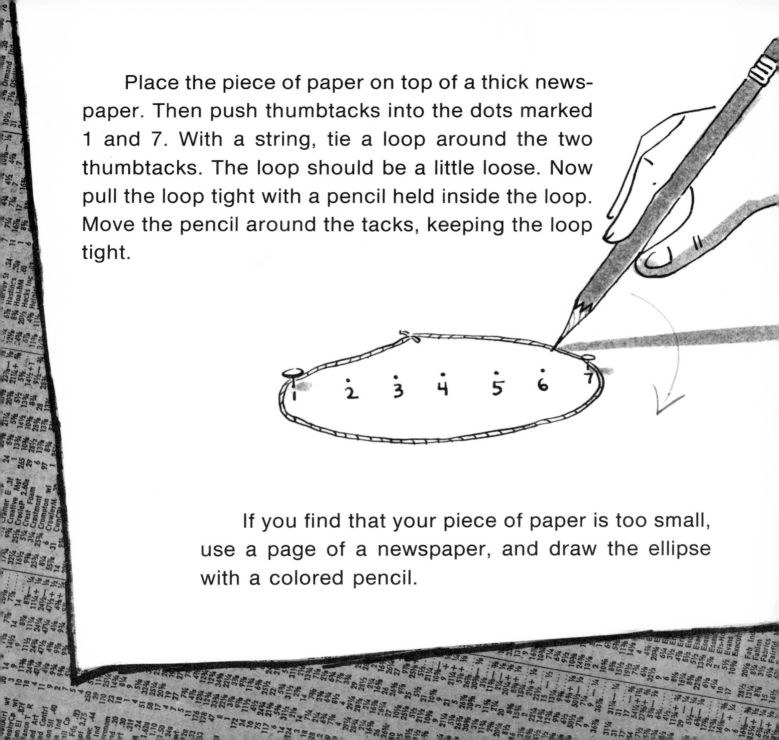

If you find that your piece of paper is too small, use a page of a newspaper, and draw the ellipse with a colored pencil.

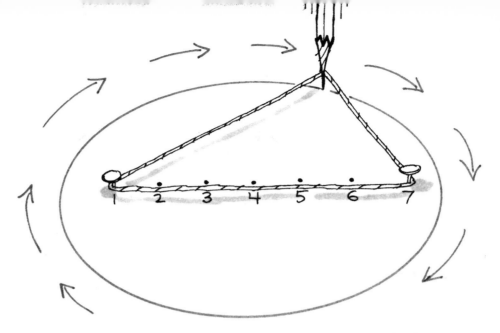

When you have moved completely around the tacks, you will have an ellipse. The position of each of the two dots into which a thumbtack was pushed is called a FOCUS of the ellipse. Every ellipse has two FOCI.

If you have two thumbtacks, a string, and a pencil, you can always draw an ellipse, using any two points as foci.

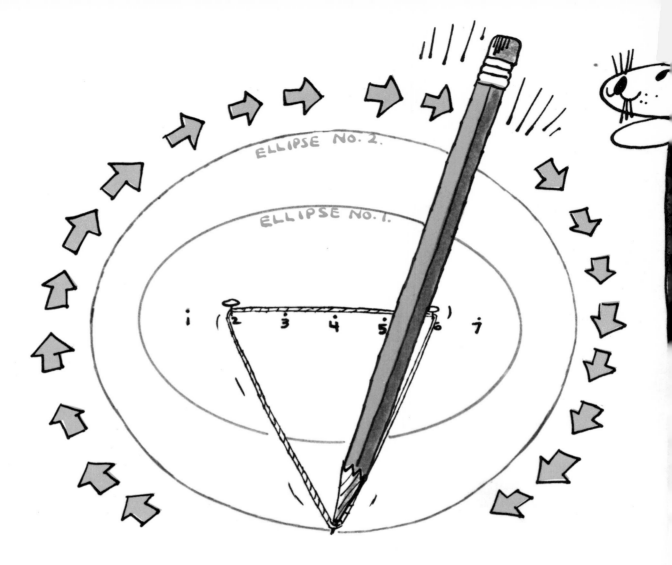

Now try moving the thumbtacks. Push them into the dots marked 2 and 6. With the same loop draw another ellipse. See how it differs from the first ellipse.

Now push the thumbtacks into the dots marked 3 and 5. With the same loop draw a third ellipse. It will look more like a circle. But it will still be an ellipse.

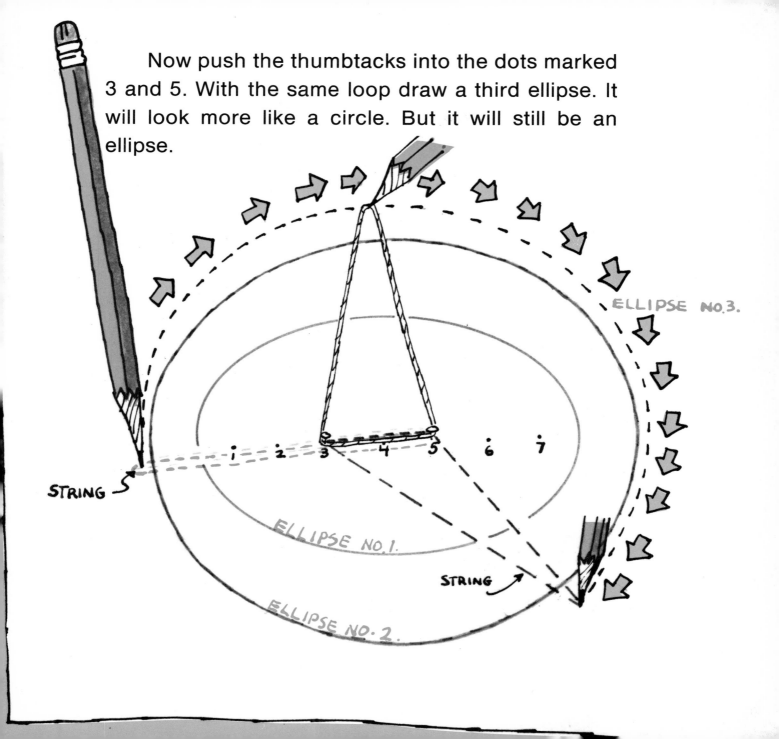

ELLIPSE NO.3.

STRING

1 2 3 4 5 6 7

ELLIPSE NO.1.

STRING

ELLIPSE NO.2.

Suppose the two thumbtacks were both pushed into the dot marked 4. Since you do not have room there for both thumbtacks, place just one thumbtack at 4. Put the same loop around the tack. Pull it tight with the pencil at the other end. When you have moved the pencil completely around the tack, you will have a circle!

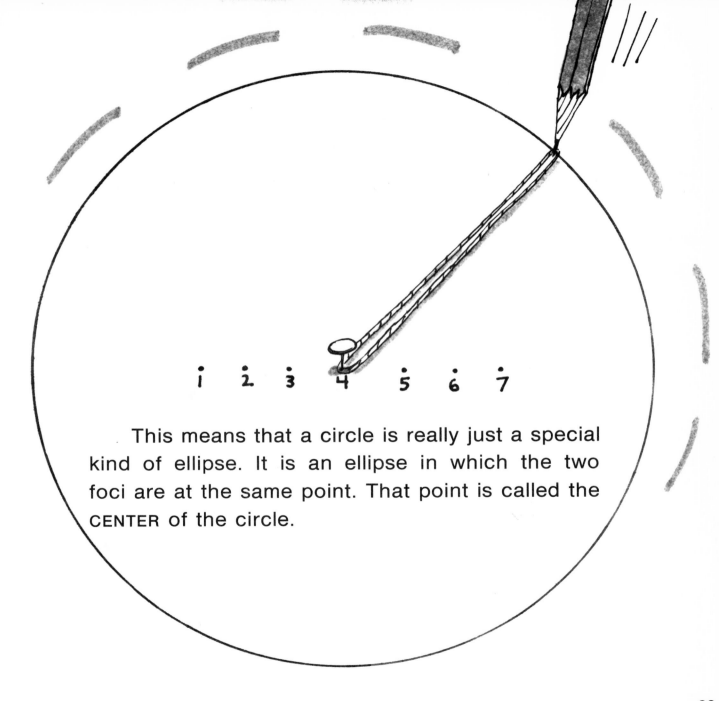

1 2 3 4 5 6 7

This means that a circle is really just a special kind of ellipse. It is an ellipse in which the two foci are at the same point. That point is called the CENTER of the circle.

In the experiments you just did, you kept the same loop but changed the positions of the thumbtacks. Let's see what happens if you keep the thumbtacks in the same places but change the size of the loop.

On a new large piece of paper make the same marks 1, 2, 3, 4, 5, 6, 7 that you did for the other experiments. Push thumbtacks into the dots marked 1 and 7. With the same loop that you have just been using, draw an ellipse. Then make a new, larger loop, but keep the thumbtacks at 1 and 7. Draw another ellipse. Again make a larger loop, keeping the thumbtacks at 1 and 7, and draw another ellipse. Keep making larger and larger loops as long as you have room on your paper for more ellipses. The ellipses will all have the same foci. They are called CONFOCAL ellipses.

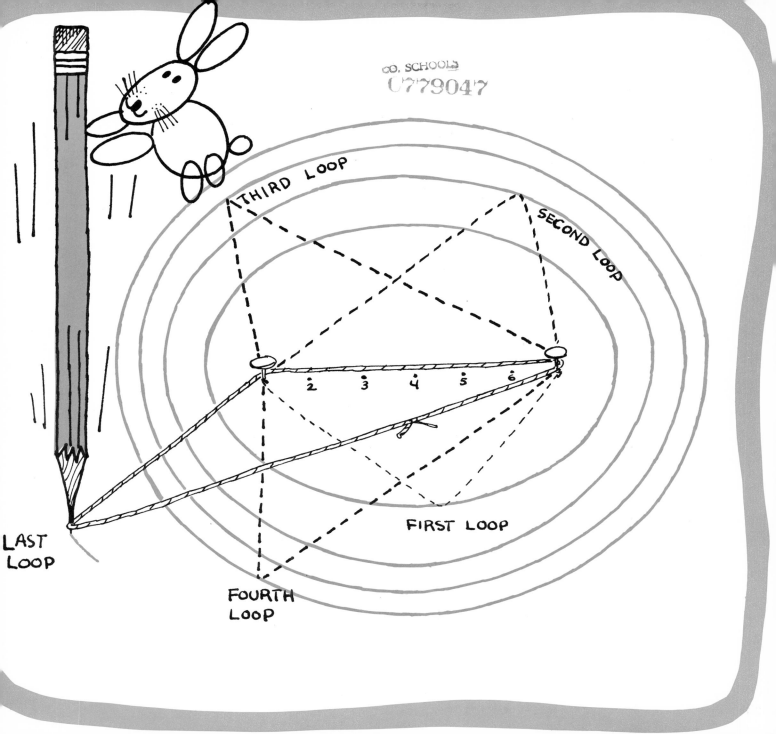

THIRD LOOP

SECOND LOOP

2 3 4 5 6

FIRST LOOP

LAST
LOOP

FOURTH
LOOP

Can you guess what will happen if you leave one tack at 1 and draw ellipses with the other tack at 7, then at 6, at 5, 4, 3, and 2? Try it.

There are ellipses in nature.
As the earth travels around the sun, its path is an ellipse.

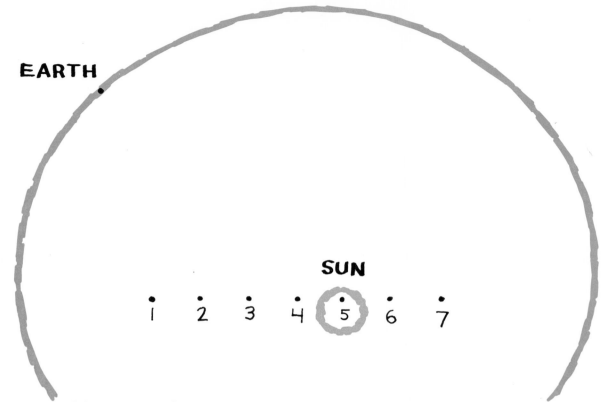

EARTH

SUN

1   2   3   4   ⑤   6   7

You can draw a picture of this.

Make marks 1, 2, 3, 4, 5, 6, 7 on a sheet of paper as you have done before. Place thumbtacks at the dots marked 3 and 5. Draw an ellipse with the same loop that you used at the very beginning. Draw a circle around the dot marked 5; label it "Sun." Now draw a much smaller circle anywhere on the ellipse; mark it "Earth."

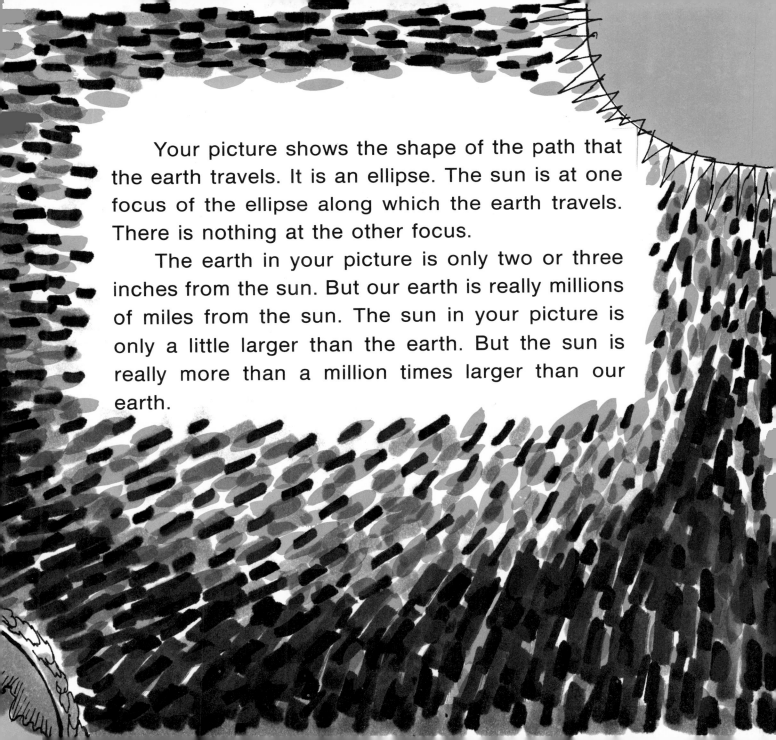

Your picture shows the shape of the path that the earth travels. It is an ellipse. The sun is at one focus of the ellipse along which the earth travels. There is nothing at the other focus.

The earth in your picture is only two or three inches from the sun. But our earth is really millions of miles from the sun. The sun in your picture is only a little larger than the earth. But the sun is really more than a million times larger than our earth.

HOLD FLASHLIGHT LIKE THIS

IMAGE ON WALL WILL LOOK LIKE THIS

CIRCLE   ELLIPSE   ELLIPSE   ELLIPSE

Here is one more experiment for you to do. In a darkened room, hold a flashlight so that its beam points directly at one wall. A circle of light will appear on the wall. If you tip the flashlight up just a little, the circle changes into an ellipse. As you continue to tip the flashlight more and more, the ellipse gets longer and longer. At a certain point the ellipse breaks open into a different shape. This new shape is called a PARABOLA. If the shape is not clear, move the flashlight closer to the wall.

As soon as you tip the flashlight a little more the parabola changes again. It gets sharper at its tip. It is now called a HYPERBOLA. As the flashlight is tipped more and more, the hyperbolas will get sharper and sharper at their tips. If the flashlight could be brought close enough to the wall, the hyperbolas would finally change into two straight lines that cross each other.

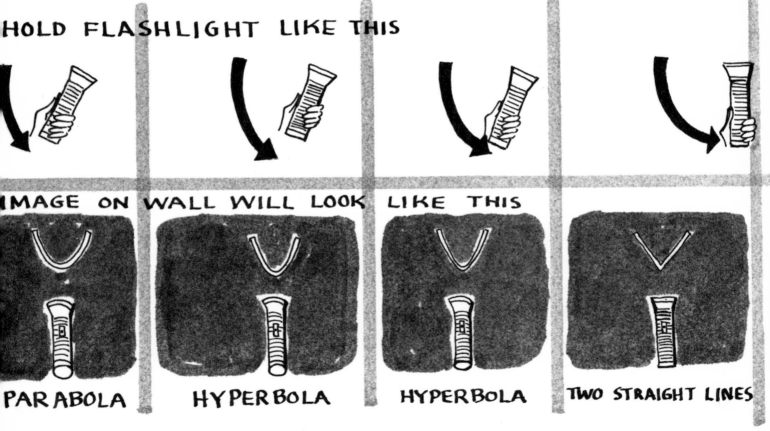

HOLD FLASHLIGHT LIKE THIS

IMAGE ON WALL WILL LOOK LIKE THIS

PARABOLA HYPERBOLA HYPERBOLA TWO STRAIGHT LINES

The changes were: CIRCLE to ELLIPSES to
PARABOLA to HYPERBOLAS to TWO STRAIGHT LINES.
They form a family of shapes.

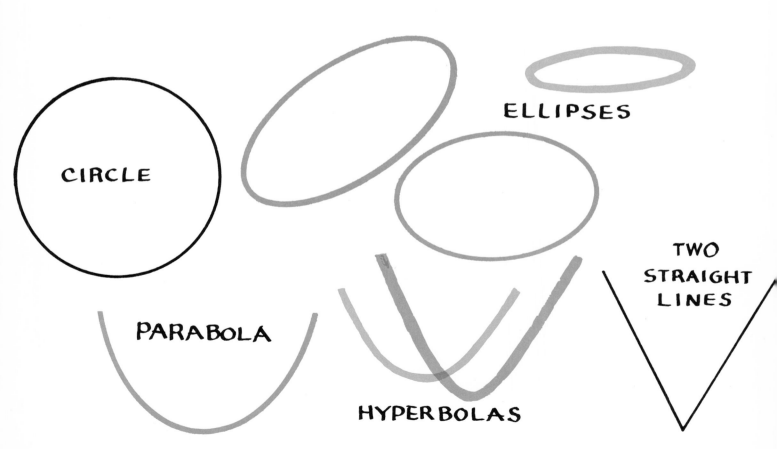

CIRCLE

ELLIPSES

PARABOLA

HYPERBOLAS

TWO
STRAIGHT
LINES

We have been learning about one member of this family: the ELLIPSE.

ABOUT THE AUTHOR

Mannis Charosh has taught mathematics to high school students for many years. He has written books, filmstrips, and motion picture narrations about mathematics and the teaching of mathematics. A chess enthusiast, Mr. Charosh is also an award-winning composer of chess problems. He now lives with his wife in Brooklyn, New York—where he has lived all of his life.

ABOUT THE ILLUSTRATOR

Leonard Kessler is a writer and illustrator of children's books as well as a designer and painter.

Mr. Kessler was born in Akron, Ohio, but he moved east to Pittsburgh at an early age. He was graduated from the Carnegie Institute of Technology with a degree in fine arts, painting, and design. Mr. Kessler enjoys playing the clarinet in his leisure time. He lives in New City, New York.